S0-DSM-591

Dukie
A gift for

Connie
From

April 23, 2004
Date

Blessed
is the
birthday
person!

Blessings on Your Birthday!

Illustrated by Melissa Babcock Saylor

Published by J. Countryman, a division of Thomas Nelson, Inc.,
Nashville, Tennessee 37214

Project editor: Terri Gibbs

Designed by Left Coast Design Inc., Portland, Oregon

ISBN: 08499-9602-3

www.thomasnelson.com

www.jcountryman.com

Printed in China

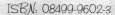

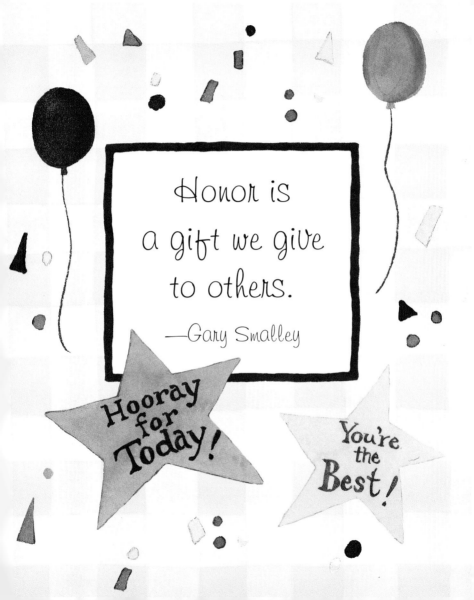

Honor is
a gift we give
to others.

—Gary Smalley

Hooray
for
Today!

You're
the
Best!

Introduction

When we bless others we give them our good wishes and prayers as a gift. We offer words of joy and kindness.

To offer a blessing for another person is to seek to give back a portion of the blessing God has given to us—as well as a portion of the blessing that person has been to us.

When we ask God to bless others, we want them to receive God's good gifts.

What is a blessing? It's a melding of remembrances, thanksgiving, heart-felt sentiment, and prayer.

It can be whimsical, witty, poignant, or prayerful. The words come straight from your heart—words of sincerity and honest affection. Write a wonderful thought for the birthday person. Wish him or her a blessed, fun-filled day!

Terri Gibbs
Editor

If you look around
and see candles,
and cake, and cheers,
and gladness,...
you can be sure
it's a birthday.

Happy moments,

Happy memories,

Happy birthday!

Have a happy

just-for-you day.

The Day of Your Birth

Date _April   1995_

Place _Thunder Bay, Ontario,_

Time of Day _the best time_

Mother _most beautiful_

Father _most handsome_

Siblings _____

_____

Your Favorites—tell who you are

List some of your favorite things:

- tuna
- donoughts
- Emily
- 4am snacks
- kittie walks
- f keces
- socializing

Your Wishes—tell who you want to became

List some of your wishes here:

- handsome
- kind
- gentle
- sensitive
- playful
- thoughtful
- compassionate

Of all the happy
things in the world,
A birthday is one
of the best!

A Birthday Blessing of Adjectives

What you are is:

S pecial

P erfect

E legant

C aring

I ntelligent

A thletic

L oving

A blessing for your birthday
today we do send,
to thank you for being
such a dear friend.
For the life you've lived and the
blessings you've bestowed
Upon each heart has brought a glow.
A glow that is shown in the love
you display,
and the fond memories now etched
in our hearts to stay.

—Yvonne Rimmer

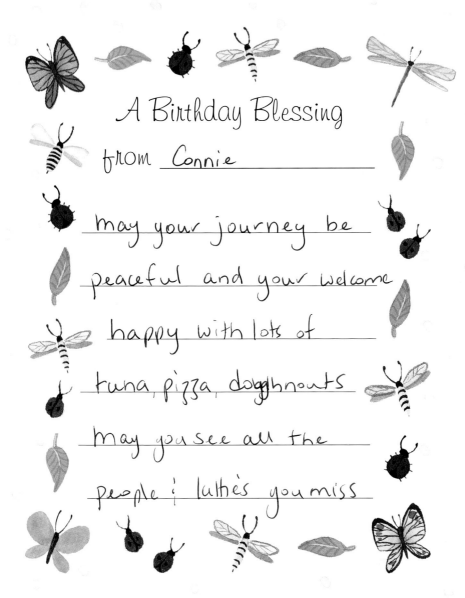

A Birthday Blessing

from __Connie__

__may your journey be__

__peaceful and your welcome__

__happy with lots of__

__tuna, pizza, doughnuts__

__may you see all the__

__people & luthies you miss__

A Birthday Blessing

from Connie

★ ★ ★

May your life have been happy and full of all the love you deserved. May you know you were always very, very, loved.

A Birthday Blessing for a Friend

You rushed into my life like a whirlwind and stirred up the dust in my mind with new insights and wisdom. You shook the cobwebs out of my heart's closets and kept my days filled with laughter and joy. May the year the Lord has already given you be packed with only fond memories, and the years to come be filled with opportunities to make rooms full of new ones. Happy Birthday!

—Natalie Nichols Gillespie

Just to be is a blessing;

Just to live is holy.

—Abraham Heschel

To build a life

is a work of art.

A Birthday Blessing

from _Connie_

May your next place be full of tall grass and lots of singing birds. May the sun shine always on your beautiful black coat with every colour of the rainbow.

The greatest happiness of life
is the conviction that we
are loved, loved for ourselves,
or rather in spite of ourselves.

—Victor Hugo

I have loved you
with an everlasting love.

Jeremiah 31:3

A Birthday Blessing

from _Connie_

May mummy be waiting
with open arms. may
she take good care of
you until I get there
may Emily find you when
her time comes.

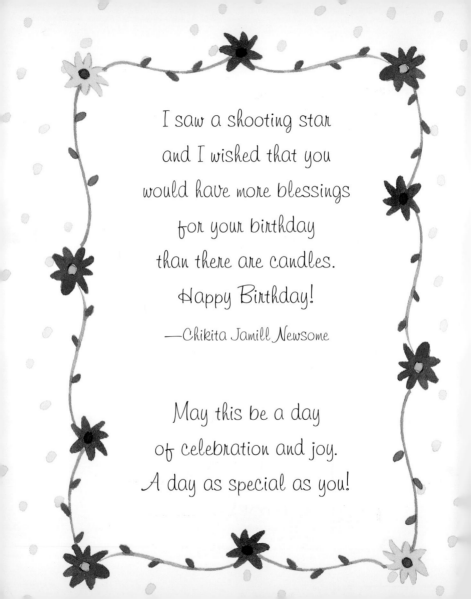

I saw a shooting star
and I wished that you
would have more blessings
for your birthday
than there are candles.
Happy Birthday!

—Chikita Jamill Newsome

May this be a day
of celebration and joy.
A day as special as you!

Instead of boring,
May your birthday
be soaring.
Instead of stressful,
May it be blissful,
Instead of dreary,
Let it be cheery!!!!!!

Have a friendly day,
as Winnie-the-Pooh would say.
A day when you relax and
enjoy the company of friends,
particularly those who are the
Fond of Eating type of friends.

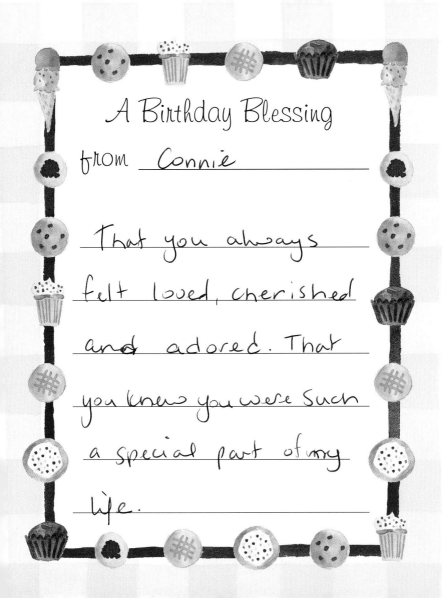

A Birthday Blessing

from _Connie_

That you always
felt loved, cherished
and adored. That
you knew you were such
a special part of my
life.

A Birthday Blessing

from_____

⭐ ⭐ ⭐

_____

_____

_____

_____

_____

_____

A touch of dotage
is a small price to pay
for a long stay on this
enchanted planet.

—Veronique Vienne

Celebrate

You're
the
Best!

Hooray
for
Today!

Happy
Day

Happy
Birthday

A Birthday Blessing

from_____

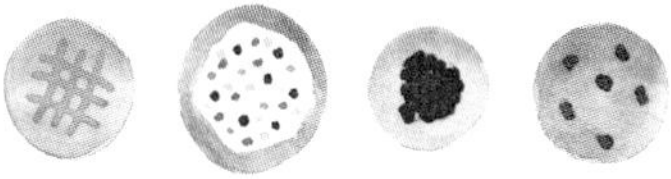

_____

_____

_____

_____

_____

_____

Have a carefree,
happy-as-can-be birthday.
And if plans go awry…
remember…
there is always room
for improvisation.

A Birthday Blessing

from_____

_____

_____

_____

_____

_____

A Birthday Blessing
for A Granddaughter

Heavenly Father, I bow in worship and praise before You...

It's about my granddaughter, whose special name is Alicia Victorene. She is just one year old. Bless her. Cause her to grow tall and healthy, by Your measure. Allow some extra angels for her, please Father. And keep the would-be giants out of her playground (life).

She curls up her feet when her daddy trys to put her down. Cause her to love You and to want always to be in Your arms. I know You will never put her down.

Love, Grandma Anne Joyce

A Birthday Blessing

from_____

_____

_____

_____

_____

_____

_____

This is the day
to say HOORAY!
For all you mean to me.
For your laughter,
you see, makes me smile.
And your love, well,
it makes life worthwhile.

I thank my God upon every remembrance of you, always in every prayer of mine making request for you...with joy.

Philippians 1:3–4

A Birthday Blessing

May time be your friend.

May the camera of your mind take many precious movies and photos of moments and events that evolve into memories.

May they renew your mind and heart with past sweetness, humor, love, and a bonding that shows both who you are and Whose you are.

May they give you strength to handle whatever life brings to you.

—Lynette Carnahan Gray

May your candles
glow brighter and
your heart be lighter
with each passing year.

The LORD bless you
and keep you;
The LORD make His face
to shine upon you, and be

gracious to you;
The LORD lift up His
countenance upon you,
and give you peace.

Numbers 6:24–26

A Birthday Blessing

from _____

_____

_____

_____

_____

_____

_____

_____

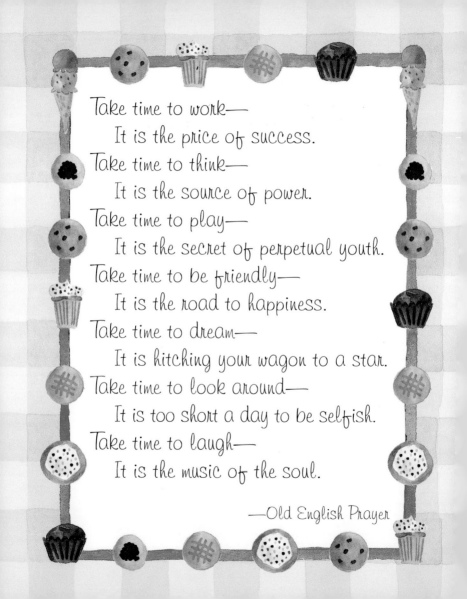

Take time to work—
   It is the price of success.
Take time to think—
   It is the source of power.
Take time to play—
   It is the secret of perpetual youth.
Take time to be friendly—
   It is the road to happiness.
Take time to dream—
   It is hitching your wagon to a star.
Take time to look around—
   It is too short a day to be selfish.
Take time to laugh—
   It is the music of the soul.

—Old English Prayer

A Birthday Blessing

from_____

_____

_____

_____

_____

_____

Write it on your heart
that every day is
the best day of the year.

—Emerson

The highest form of bliss is living
with a certain degree of folly.

—Erasmus

A Birthday Blessing for YOU!

May your birthday be blessed with more than CAKE, CANDLES, and SONG. May it be the beginning of another year of opportunities to praise God, serve your fellow man, and improve yourself. May your cake, candles, and song not represent a date on the calendar but a destiny for eternity.

—Lynette Carnahan Gray

A Birthday Blessing

from_____

_____

_____

_____

_____

_____

_____

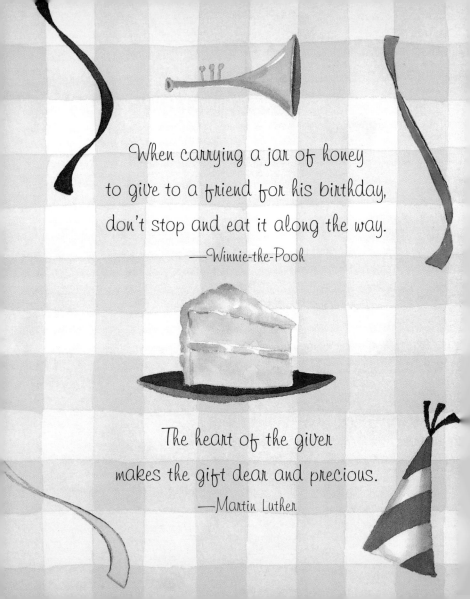

When carrying a jar of honey
to give to a friend for his birthday,
don't stop and eat it along the way.
—Winnie-the-Pooh

The heart of the giver
makes the gift dear and precious.
—Martin Luther

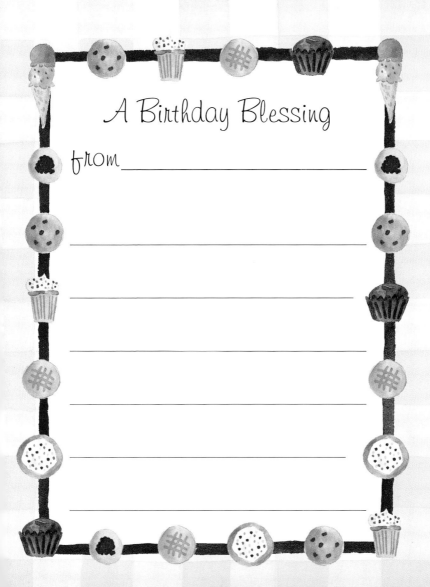

A Birthday Blessing

from_____

_____

_____

_____

_____

_____

_____

A Birthday Blessing

from_____

_____

_____

_____

_____

_____

_____

One, two,
three,
Between you and me,
I hope this day is happy—
As happy as can be!

A Birthday Blessing

from _____

_____

_____

_____

_____

_____

A Birthday Blessing

from _____

_____

_____

_____

_____

_____

_____

God made the sun
And God made the tree,
God made the mountains
And God made me.

I thank you, O God,
For the sun and the tree,
For making the mountains
And for making me.

—Leah Gale

Why are birthdays so enchanting to a child? Beside this single event every other holiday pales.... For the youngster having the birthday is indeed king or queen. Special from the moment of waking. His eyes sparkle. He walks in a proud new way....

And he must ask, no matter how often you've told him, "What time was I born?" And his face wears a special wonder as you explain. He ponders the remarkable fact of his being. How exciting!...

Oh, to retain that early fervor for living. That first rosy blush of being in love with life itself.

—Marjorie Holmes

A Birthday Blessing

from _____

_____

_____

_____

_____

_____

A book of birthday blessings
For someone totally special.
Who could that be...but you?

I pray for God's best,
Add warmest thoughts,
And send special wishes, too!

A Birthday Blessing

from _____

_____

_____

_____

_____

_____

surprises

laughter

friends

Have a day
filled with
happy things.

balloons

fun

family

giggles

It's more than a birthday. It's a celebration!

You're the Best!
Celebrate
Hooray for Today!
Happy Day
Happy Birthday

If stars were good wishes,
And the moon, too,
I'd wish for a night full
Of sky just for you!

A Birthday Blessing

from_____

Birthday Rules:

1. Have fun
2. Wish big
3. Laugh
4. Be suspect of suspicious
   surprises
5. Be happy
6. Never count the candles
7. Enjoy the day in every way

The days that
make us happy
make us wise.

—John Masefield

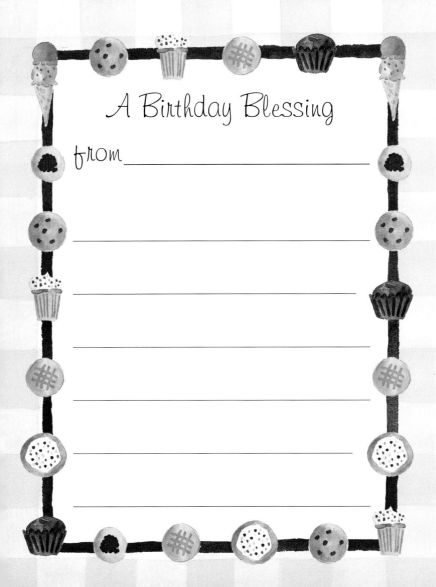

A Birthday Blessing

from_____

_____

_____

_____

_____

_____

_____

A Birthday Prayer

God made today,
And God made me.
For His blessings I pray,
And His child to be.

A Birthday Blessing

from_____

_____

_____

_____

_____

_____

_____

A Birthday Blessing

from_____

_____

_____

_____

_____

_____

_____

When it's your birthday,
this is what to do.
Get up in the morning,
and say
"Yahooooooo!"

The best birthday gifts are free:

Smiles

Laughter

Compliments

Happy Birthday

Hugs

Kisses

Joy

How precious...are Your thoughts to me, O God! How great is the sum of them! If I should count them, they would be more in number than the sand.

Psalm 139:17–18

God Thinks You're Special

If God had a refrigerator, your picture would be on it.

If He had a wallet, your photo would be in it.

He sends you flowers every spring and a sunrise every morning.

Whenever you want to talk, He'll listen.

He can live anywhere in the universe, and He chose your heart. . . .

Face it, friend. He's crazy about you.

—Max Lucado

May your birthday be a fun-in-the-sun sort of day.

A Wish for Every Candle on the Cake

Here are some things I wish for you:

The gift of _peace_

Because _I love you_

The gift of _love_

Because _I love you_

The gift of _chicken pizza_

Because _I love you_

The gift of _letting you go_

Because _I love you_

A Birthday Blessing

from _____

_____

_____

_____

_____

_____

_____

A Birthday Blessing

from _____

_____

_____

_____

_____

_____

Have a happy
just-for-you day.